Change the Narrative:

Goal-Setting Journal

Manifest the life you want.

November Media Publishing, Chicago IL.

LaKeshia Hampton keshia_hamp22@comcast.net

Ordering Information: Special discounts are available on quantity purchases by corporations, associations, and others. For details, contact the publisher at the email address above.

Printed in the United States of America

Published by November Media Publishing

ISBN: 9781087987385 (Paperback)

First Edition: September 2021

10 9 8 7 6 5 4 3 2 1

Introduction

If you are reading this, you are probably one of many who has visions and dreams but is not exactly sure how to achieve them—whether that is starting a new business, writing a book, going back to school or losing weight. If you are anything like me, you are probably a big procrastinator. If not, good for you! LOL. No, seriously. Is it getting out of hand? Are you waiting for the "perfect moment" or waiting for when Jesus returns? Sis, seriously, we need to get this together!

To live the best life that everyone talks about, you have to do some inventory and begin to manifest things to existence. We all wait until the New Year to write our goals, have vision board parties, etc. And do not get me wrong - all those things are great. However, what steps are you taking on a daily basis to reach your goals?

During this pandemic, I developed so much anxiety and fear and felt defeated at certain moments. It appeared like my world was getting smaller and my dreams further and further out of reach. I knew I needed to make a difference. As women, we are groomed to be super. We are groomed to carry heavy weight—all while still getting things done. But we are HUMAN. We deserve to be extraordinary without being left on empty. During this journey, I started a self-care journal and went on a 30-day fast. It was the best decision I made. My goals were simple, like waking up early to meditate or pray, reading for 30 minutes or exercising twice a week. I also wrote daily affirmations, listened to motivational videos and/or did things that made me happy. It seems simple, but I was glad I afforded myself the space and time. I do not have everything figured out.

But I feel prepared to continue the journey.

I live my life working to make each and every day better than the previous one. I stand in the gap for so many women, because I am a witness that life still goes on, regardless of past failures, traumatic experiences or failed relationships. Everyone has a story to tell. But are you willing to CHANGE THE NARRATIVE, BE AUTHENTIC and MANIFEST THE LIFE YOU WANT?

If you picked up this journal and made it this far, I assume you are a dreamer, or you have some goals you want to achieve, or you are looking for an accountability partner or for some self-motivation. Either way, this journal is for you.

This journal will include affirmation quotes, daily encouragement, goal setting and creative space.

My overall goal in creating this journal is to encourage, engage and equip others to believe in the possibilities and live the lives they would if they only knew how.

"Fight the Struggle with the Vision"

90 Day Focus

What do you want to accomplish by the end of 90 Days?

_____

_____

_____

_____

_____

_____

_____

_____

_____

_____

_____

_____

_____

_____

_____

_____

_____

_____

_____

_____

_____

_____

Self-Care Plan

List 5 things you want to do for yourself over the next 90 days?

_____

_____

_____

_____

_____

_____

_____

_____

_____

_____

_____

_____

_____

_____

_____

_____

_____

_____

_____

_____

_____

_____

_____

_____

Day 1

Morning Affirmation

Today, I am grateful for... _____

_____

_____

_____

What I learned from yesterday... _____

_____

_____

_____

As a reminder, my 90-day goal is to... _____

_____

_____

Why is this goal important? _____

_____

_____

Three realistic steps that I can take towards this goal today are...

1. _____

2. _____

3. _____

Day 1

Did I achieve my goals for today? If not, did I make progress?

_____

_____

How do I feel now that I have completed (or not completed) this goal?

_____

_____

What three things will you no longer accept?

1. _____
2. _____
3. _____

What are 3 prayers that I have for today?

1. _____
2. _____
3. _____

Today, I release ... _____

_____

For the Spirit God gave us does not make us timid, but gives us power, love and self-discipline.

- 2 TIMOTHY 1:7

Day 2

Did I achieve my goals for today? If not, did I make progress?

_____

_____

How do I feel now that I have completed (or not completed) this goal?

_____

_____

What three things will you no longer accept?

1. _____
2. _____
3. _____

What are 3 prayers that I have for today?

1. _____
2. _____
3. _____

Today, I release ... _____

_____

Day 2

Today, I am grateful for... _____

_____

_____

_____

What I learned from yesterday... _____

_____

_____

_____

As a reminder, my 90-day goal is to... _____

_____

_____

Why is this goal important? _____

_____

_____

Three realistic steps that I can take towards this goal today are...

1. _____
2. _____
3. _____

I ACCEPT MYSELF EXACTLY

as I am

Day 3

Morning Affirmation

Today, I am grateful for... _____

_____

_____

_____

What I learned from yesterday... _____

_____

_____

_____

As a reminder, my 90-day goal is to... _____

_____

_____

Why is this goal important? _____

_____

_____

Three realistic steps that I can take towards this goal today are...

1. _____

2. _____

3. _____

Day 3

Did I achieve my goals for today? If not, did I make progress?

_____

_____

How do I feel now that I have completed (or not completed) this goal?

_____

_____

What three things will you no longer accept?

1. _____
2. _____
3. _____

What are 3 prayers that I have for today?

1. _____
2. _____
3. _____

Today, I release ... _____

_____

THE MORE I LOVE MYSELF, THE MORE I GIVE TO OTHERS.

Day 4

Today, I am grateful for... _____

_____

_____

_____

What I learned from yesterday... _____

_____

_____

_____

As a reminder, my 90-day goal is to... _____

_____

_____

Why is this goal important? _____

_____

_____

Three realistic steps that I can take towards this goal today are...

1. _____

2. _____

3. _____

Day 4

Evening Affirmation

Did I achieve my goals for today? If not, did I make progress?

_____

_____

How do I feel now that I have completed (or not completed) this goal?

_____

_____

What three things will you no longer accept?
1. _____
2. _____
3. _____

What are 3 prayers that I have for today?
1. _____
2. _____
3. _____

Today, I release ... _____

_____

MY THOUGHTS
TODAY
CREATE

my future prosperity.

Day 5

Morning Affirmation

Today, I am grateful for... _____

_____

_____

_____

What I learned from yesterday... _____

_____

_____

_____

As a reminder, my 90-day goal is to... _____

_____

_____

Why is this goal important? _____

_____

_____

Three realistic steps that I can take towards this goal today are...

1. _____
2. _____
3. _____

Day 5

Evening Affirmation

Did I achieve my goals for today? If not, did I make progress?

_____

_____

How do I feel now that I have completed (or not completed) this goal?

_____

_____

What three things will you no longer accept?
1. _____
2. _____
3. _____

What are 3 prayers that I have for today?
1. _____
2. _____
3. _____

Today, I release ... _____

_____

I AM LOOKING FORWARD TO ALL THE NEW CHANGES IN MY LIFE.

Day 6

Today, I am grateful for... _____

_____

_____

_____

What I learned from yesterday... _____

_____

_____

_____

As a reminder, my 90-day goal is to... _____

_____

_____

Why is this goal important? _____

_____

_____

Three realistic steps that I can take towards this goal today are...

1. _____
2. _____
3. _____

Day 6

Did I achieve my goals for today? If not, did I make progress?

_____

_____

How do I feel now that I have completed (or not completed) this goal?

_____

_____

What three things will you no longer accept?

1. _____
2. _____
3. _____

What are 3 prayers that I have for today?

1. _____
2. _____
3. _____

Today, I release ... _____

_____

I AM FALLING IN LOVE WITH TAKING CARE OF MYSELF.

Day 7

Morning Affirmation

Today, I am grateful for... _____
_____
_____
_____

What I learned from yesterday... _____
_____
_____
_____

As a reminder, my 90-day goal is to... _____
_____
_____

Why is this goal important? _____
_____
_____

Three realistic steps that I can take towards this goal today are...

1. _____
2. _____
3. _____

Day 7

Did I achieve my goals for today? If not, did I make progress?

_____

_____

How do I feel now that I have completed (or not completed) this goal?

_____

_____

What three things will you no longer accept?

1. _____
2. _____
3. _____

What are 3 prayers that I have for today?

1. _____
2. _____
3. _____

Today, I release ... _____

_____

I AM GRATEFUL FOR ALL *people* IN MY LIFE.

Day 8

Morning Affirmation

Today, I am grateful for... _____

_____

_____

_____

What I learned from yesterday... _____

_____

_____

_____

As a reminder, my 90-day goal is to... _____

_____

_____

Why is this goal important? _____

_____

_____

Three realistic steps that I can take towards this goal today are...

1. _____

2. _____

3. _____

Day 8

Evening Affirmation

Did I achieve my goals for today? If not, did I make progress?

_____

_____

How do I feel now that I have completed (or not completed) this goal?

_____

_____

What three things will you no longer accept?

1. _____

2. _____

3. _____

What are 3 prayers that I have for today?

1. _____

2. _____

3. _____

Today, I release ... _____

_____

EVERY DAY,

in every way.

I AM
GROWING.

Day 9

Morning Affirmation

Today, I am grateful for... _____

_____

_____

_____

What I learned from yesterday... _____

_____

_____

_____

As a reminder, my 90-day goal is to... _____

_____

_____

Why is this goal important? _____

_____

_____

Three realistic steps that I can take towards this goal today are...

1. _____
2. _____
3. _____

Day 9

Evening Affirmation

Did I achieve my goals for today? If not, did I make progress?

_____

_____

How do I feel now that I have completed (or not completed) this goal?

_____

_____

What three things will you no longer accept?

1. _____

2. _____

3. _____

What are 3 prayers that I have for today?

1. _____

2. _____

3. _____

Today, I release ... _____

_____

THIS FEELING

will pass

Day 10

Today, I am grateful for... _____

_____

_____

_____

What I learned from yesterday... _____

_____

_____

_____

As a reminder, my 90-day goal is to..._____

_____

_____

Why is this goal important?_____

_____

_____

Three realistic steps that I can take towards this goal today are...

1. _____

2. _____

3. _____

Day 10

Did I achieve my goals for today? If not, did I make progress?

_____

_____

How do I feel now that I have completed (or not completed) this goal?

_____

_____

What three things will you no longer accept?

1. _____
2. _____
3. _____

What are 3 prayers that I have for today?

1. _____
2. _____
3. _____

Today, I release ... _____

_____

True love comes from within.

Day 11

Today, I am grateful for... _____

_____

_____

_____

What I learned from yesterday... _____

_____

_____

_____

As a reminder, my 90-day goal is to... _____

_____

_____

Why is this goal important? _____

_____

_____

Three realistic steps that I can take towards this goal today are...

1. _____
2. _____
3. _____

Day 11

Evening Affirmation

Did I achieve my goals for today? If not, did I make progress?

_____

_____

How do I feel now that I have completed (or not completed) this goal?

_____

_____

What three things will you no longer accept?

1. _____
2. _____
3. _____

What are 3 prayers that I have for today?

1. _____
2. _____
3. _____

Today, I release ... _____

_____

EVERYTHING THAT I NEED WILL BE PROVIDED TO ME AT THE RIGHT TIME AND AT THE RIGHT PLACE.

Day 12

Today, I am grateful for... _____

_____

_____

_____

_____

What I learned from yesterday... _____

_____

_____

_____

As a reminder, my 90-day goal is to... _____

_____

_____

Why is this goal important? _____

_____

_____

Three realistic steps that I can take towards this goal today are...

1. _____

2. _____

3. _____

Day 12

Did I achieve my goals for today? If not, did I make progress?

_____

_____

How do I feel now that I have completed (or not completed)
this goal?

_____

_____

What three things will you no longer accept?

1. _____

2. _____

3. _____

What are 3 prayers that I have for today?

1. _____

2. _____

3. _____

Today, I release ... _____

_____

TODAY THE SUN IS SHINING

for me.

Morning Affirmation

Today, I am grateful for... _____

_____

_____

_____

What I learned from yesterday... _____

_____

_____

_____

As a reminder, my 90-day goal is to... _____

_____

_____

Why is this goal important? _____

_____

_____

Three realistic steps that I can take towards this goal today are...

1. _____
2. _____
3. _____

Day 13

Evening Affirmation

Did I achieve my goals for today? If not, did I make progress?

_____

_____

How do I feel now that I have completed (or not completed) this goal?

_____

_____

What three things will you no longer accept?

1. _____
2. _____
3. _____

What are 3 prayers that I have for today?

1. _____
2. _____
3. _____

Today, I release ... _____

_____

Day 14

Today, I am grateful for... _____

_____

_____

_____

What I learned from yesterday... _____

_____

_____

_____

As a reminder, my 90-day goal is to... _____

_____

_____

Why is this goal important? _____

_____

_____

Three realistic steps that I can take towards this goal today are...

1. _____

2. _____

3. _____

Day 14

Did I achieve my goals for today? If not, did I make progress?

_____

_____

How do I feel now that I have completed (or not completed) this goal?

_____

_____

What three things will you no longer accept?

1. _____
2. _____
3. _____

What are 3 prayers that I have for today?

1. _____
2. _____
3. _____

Today, I release ... _____

_____

GIVING UP IS NOT AN OPTION!

Day 15

Morning Affirmation

Today, I am grateful for... _____

_____

_____

_____

What I learned from yesterday... _____

_____

_____

_____

As a reminder, my 90-day goal is to... _____

_____

_____

Why is this goal important? _____

_____

_____

Three realistic steps that I can take towards this goal today are...

1. _____

2. _____

3. _____

Day 15

Evening Affirmation

Did I achieve my goals for today? If not, did I make progress?

_____

_____

How do I feel now that I have completed (or not completed) this goal?

_____

_____

What three things will you no longer accept?

1. _____

2. _____

3. _____

What are 3 prayers that I have for today?

1. _____

2. _____

3. _____

Today, I release ... _____

_____

YOU
ARE
VALUED.

Day 16

Today, I am grateful for... _____

_____

_____

_____

What I learned from yesterday... _____

_____

_____

_____

As a reminder, my 90-day goal is to... _____

_____

_____

Why is this goal important? _____

_____

_____

Three realistic steps that I can take towards this goal today are...

1. _____

2. _____

3. _____

Day 16

Did I achieve my goals for today? If not, did I make progress?

_____

_____

How do I feel now that I have completed (or not completed) this goal?

_____

_____

What three things will you no longer accept?

1. _____
2. _____
3. _____

What are 3 prayers that I have for today?

1. _____
2. _____
3. _____

Today, I release ... _____

_____

I HAVE THE COURAGE TO CHANGE THE WAY I THINK.

Day 17

Morning Affirmation

Today, I am grateful for... _____
_____
_____
_____

What I learned from yesterday... _____
_____
_____
_____

As a reminder, my 90-day goal is to..._____
_____
_____

Why is this goal important?_____
_____
_____

Three realistic steps that I can take towards this goal today are...

1. _____
2. _____
3. _____

Day 17

Did I achieve my goals for today? If not, did I make progress?

_____

_____

How do I feel now that I have completed (or not completed) this goal?

_____

_____

What three things will you no longer accept?

1. _____
2. _____
3. _____

What are 3 prayers that I have for today?

1. _____
2. _____
3. _____

Today, I release ... _____

_____

I am
SUCCESSFUL.

Day 18

Morning Affirmation

Today, I am grateful for... _____

_____

_____

_____

What I learned from yesterday... _____

_____

_____

_____

As a reminder, my 90-day goal is to... _____

_____

_____

Why is this goal important? _____

_____

_____

Three realistic steps that I can take towards this goal today are...

1. _____

2. _____

3. _____

Day 18

Evening Affirmation

Did I achieve my goals for today? If not, did I make progress?

_____

_____

How do I feel now that I have completed (or not completed) this goal?

_____

_____

What three things will you no longer accept?

1. _____
2. _____
3. _____

What are 3 prayers that I have for today?

1. _____
2. _____
3. _____

Today, I release ... _____

_____

Day 19

Today, I am grateful for... _____
_____
_____
_____

What I learned from yesterday... _____
_____
_____
_____

As a reminder, my 90-day goal is to... _____
_____
_____

Why is this goal important? _____
_____
_____

Three realistic steps that I can take towards this goal today are...

1. _____
2. _____
3. _____

Day 19

Did I achieve my goals for today? If not, did I make progress?

_____

_____

How do I feel now that I have completed (or not completed)
this goal?

_____

_____

What three things will you no longer accept?

1. _____
2. _____
3. _____

What are 3 prayers that I have for today?

1. _____
2. _____
3. _____

Today, I release ... _____

_____

Day 20

Today, I am grateful for... _____

_____

_____

_____

What I learned from yesterday... _____

_____

_____

_____

As a reminder, my 90-day goal is to..._____

_____

_____

Why is this goal important? _____

_____

_____

Three realistic steps that I can take towards this goal today are...

1. _____

2. _____

3. _____

Day 20

Evening Affirmation

Did I achieve my goals for today? If not, did I make progress?

_____

_____

How do I feel now that I have completed (or not completed) this goal?

_____

_____

What three things will you no longer accept?

1. _____
2. _____
3. _____

What are 3 prayers that I have for today?

1. _____
2. _____
3. _____

Today, I release ... _____

_____

I AM
DEDICATED
TO BUILDING
MY DESIRED
future.

Day 21

Today, I am grateful for... _____

_____

_____

_____

What I learned from yesterday... _____

_____

_____

_____

As a reminder, my 90-day goal is to... _____

_____

_____

Why is this goal important? _____

_____

_____

Three realistic steps that I can take towards this goal today are...

1. _____

2. _____

3. _____

Day 21

Did I achieve my goals for today? If not, did I make progress?

_____

_____

How do I feel now that I have completed (or not completed) this goal?

_____

_____

What three things will you no longer accept?

1. _____

2. _____

3. _____

What are 3 prayers that I have for today?

1. _____

2. _____

3. _____

Today, I release … _____

_____

EVERYTHING I AM GOING THROUGH IS INSTILLING IN ME SOMETHING VALUABLE.

Day 22

Morning Affirmation

Today, I am grateful for... _____

_____

_____

_____

What I learned from yesterday... _____

_____

_____

_____

As a reminder, my 90-day goal is to... _____

_____

_____

Why is this goal important? _____

_____

_____

Three realistic steps that I can take towards this goal today are...

1. _____
2. _____
3. _____

Day 22

Did I achieve my goals for today? If not, did I make progress?

_____

_____

How do I feel now that I have completed (or not completed) this goal?

_____

_____

What three things will you no longer accept?

1. _____

2. _____

3. _____

What are 3 prayers that I have for today?

1. _____

2. _____

3. _____

Today, I release ... _____

_____

I AM DESTINED FOR GREATNESS!

Day 23

Today, I am grateful for... _____

_____

_____

_____

What I learned from yesterday... _____

_____

_____

_____

As a reminder, my 90-day goal is to..._____

_____

_____

Why is this goal important? _____

_____

_____

Three realistic steps that I can take towards this goal today are...

1. _____

2. _____

3. _____

Day 23

Did I achieve my goals for today? If not, did I make progress?

_____

_____

How do I feel now that I have completed (or not completed) this goal?

_____

_____

What three things will you no longer accept?

1. _____
2. _____
3. _____

What are 3 prayers that I have for today?

1. _____
2. _____
3. _____

Today, I release … _____

_____

I OPEN THE DOOR FOR SOMETHING

better.

Day 24

Today, I am grateful for... _____

_____

_____

_____

What I learned from yesterday... _____

_____

_____

_____

As a reminder, my 90-day goal is to... _____

_____

_____

Why is this goal important? _____

_____

_____

Three realistic steps that I can take towards this goal today are...

1. _____
2. _____
3. _____

Day 24

Evening Affirmation

Did I achieve my goals for today? If not, did I make progress?

_____

_____

How do I feel now that I have completed (or not completed) this goal?

_____

_____

What three things will you no longer accept?

1. _____
2. _____
3. _____

What are 3 prayers that I have for today?

1. _____
2. _____
3. _____

Today, I release ... _____

_____

I AM

healing

Day 25

Today, I am grateful for... _____

_____

_____

_____

What I learned from yesterday... _____

_____

_____

_____

As a reminder, my 90-day goal is to..._____

_____

_____

Why is this goal important?_____

_____

_____

Three realistic steps that I can take towards this goal today are...

1. _____

2. _____

3. _____

Day 25

Did I achieve my goals for today? If not, did I make progress?

_____

_____

How do I feel now that I have completed (or not completed) this goal?

_____

_____

What three things will you no longer accept?

1. _____

2. _____

3. _____

What are 3 prayers that I have for today?

1. _____

2. _____

3. _____

Today, I release ... _____

_____

NONE OF MY FEARS CAN GO WHERE I AM

headed.

Day 26

Today, I am grateful for... _____
_____
_____
_____

What I learned from yesterday... _____
_____
_____
_____

As a reminder, my 90-day goal is to... _____
_____
_____

Why is this goal important? _____
_____
_____

Three realistic steps that I can take towards this goal today are...

1. _____
2. _____
3. _____

Day 26

Evening Affirmation

Did I achieve my goals for today? If not, did I make progress?

_____

_____

How do I feel now that I have completed (or not completed) this goal?

_____

_____

What three things will you no longer accept?

1. _____

2. _____

3. _____

What are 3 prayers that I have for today?

1. _____

2. _____

3. _____

Today, I release ... _____

_____

DON'T BE AFRAID. BE FOCUSED. BE DETERMINED. BE HOPEFUL. BE EMPOWERED.

Michelle Obama

Day 27

Today, I am grateful for... _____

_____

_____

_____

What I learned from yesterday... _____

_____

_____

_____

As a reminder, my 90-day goal is to... _____

_____

_____

Why is this goal important? _____

_____

_____

Three realistic steps that I can take towards this goal today are...

1. _____

2. _____

3. _____

Day 27

Did I achieve my goals for today? If not, did I make progress?

_____

_____

How do I feel now that I have completed (or not completed) this goal?

_____

_____

What three things will you no longer accept?

1. _____

2. _____

3. _____

What are 3 prayers that I have for today?

1. _____

2. _____

3. _____

Today, I release ... _____

_____

I CAN DO ALL THINGS THROUGH CHRIST, WHO STRENGTHENS ME.

-PHILIPPIANS 4:13

Day 28

Today, I am grateful for... _____

_____

_____

_____

What I learned from yesterday... _____

_____

_____

_____

As a reminder, my 90-day goal is to..._____

_____

_____

Why is this goal important? _____

_____

_____

Three realistic steps that I can take towards this goal today are...

1. _____

2. _____

3. _____

Day 28

Evening Affirmation

Did I achieve my goals for today? If not, did I make progress?

_____

_____

How do I feel now that I have completed (or not completed) this goal?

_____

_____

What three things will you no longer accept?

1. _____
2. _____
3. _____

What are 3 prayers that I have for today?

1. _____
2. _____
3. _____

Today, I release ... _____

_____

WRITE THE VISION AND MAKE PLAIN.

-HABAKKUK 2:2

Day 29

Morning Affirmation

Today, I am grateful for... _____

_____

_____

_____

What I learned from yesterday... _____

_____

_____

_____

As a reminder, my 90-day goal is to... _____

_____

_____

Why is this goal important? _____

_____

_____

Three realistic steps that I can take towards this goal today are...

1. _____

2. _____

3. _____

Day 29

Did I achieve my goals for today? If not, did I make progress?

_____

_____

How do I feel now that I have completed (or not completed) this goal?

_____

_____

What three things will you no longer accept?

1. _____
2. _____
3. _____

What are 3 prayers that I have for today?

1. _____
2. _____
3. _____

Today, I release ... _____

_____

I am
MORE THAN
MY FLAWS -
I am
ALSO MY
STRENGTHS.

Day 30

Today, I am grateful for... _____

_____

_____

_____

What I learned from yesterday... _____

_____

_____

_____

As a reminder, my 90-day goal is to... _____

_____

_____

Why is this goal important? _____

_____

_____

Three realistic steps that I can take towards this goal today are...

1. _____

2. _____

3. _____

Day 30

Evening Affirmation

Did I achieve my goals for today? If not, did I make progress?

_____

_____

How do I feel now that I have completed (or not completed) this goal?

_____

_____

What three things will you no longer accept?

1. _____
2. _____
3. _____

What are 3 prayers that I have for today?

1. _____
2. _____
3. _____

Today, I release ... _____

_____

Day 31

Today, I am grateful for... _____

_____

_____

_____

What I learned from yesterday... _____

_____

_____

_____

As a reminder, my 90-day goal is to... _____

_____

_____

Why is this goal important? _____

_____

_____

Three realistic steps that I can take towards this goal today are...

1. _____
2. _____
3. _____

Day 31

Evening Affirmation

Did I achieve my goals for today? If not, did I make progress?

_____

_____

How do I feel now that I have completed (or not completed) this goal?

_____

_____

What three things will you no longer accept?
1. _____
2. _____
3. _____

What are 3 prayers that I have for today?
1. _____
2. _____
3. _____

Today, I release ... _____

_____

I'M FOCUSED ON THE POSITIVE AND THAT'S THE ONLY THING THAT MATTERS RIGHT NOW.

Day 32

Today, I am grateful for... _____
_____
_____
_____

What I learned from yesterday... _____
_____
_____
_____

As a reminder, my 90-day goal is to... _____
_____
_____

Why is this goal important? _____
_____
_____

Three realistic steps that I can take towards this goal today are...

1. _____
2. _____
3. _____

Day 32

Evening Affirmation

Did I achieve my goals for today? If not, did I make progress?

_____

_____

How do I feel now that I have completed (or not completed) this goal?

_____

_____

What three things will you no longer accept?

1. _____
2. _____
3. _____

What are 3 prayers that I have for today?

1. _____
2. _____
3. _____

Today, I release ... _____

_____

I AM BEYOND MY ANXIETY!

Day 33

Today, I am grateful for... _____

_____

_____

_____

What I learned from yesterday... _____

_____

_____

_____

As a reminder, my 90-day goal is to... _____

_____

_____

Why is this goal important? _____

_____

_____

Three realistic steps that I can take towards this goal today are...

1. _____
2. _____
3. _____

Day 33

Evening Affirmation

Did I achieve my goals for today? If not, did I make progress?

_____

_____

How do I feel now that I have completed (or not completed) this goal?

_____

_____

What three things will you no longer accept?

1. _____
2. _____
3. _____

What are 3 prayers that I have for today?

1. _____
2. _____
3. _____

Today, I release ... _____

_____

Day 34

Today, I am grateful for... _____

_____

_____

_____

What I learned from yesterday... _____

_____

_____

_____

As a reminder, my 90-day goal is to... _____

_____

_____

Why is this goal important? _____

_____

_____

Three realistic steps that I can take towards this goal today are...

1. _____

2. _____

3. _____

Day 34

Evening Affirmation

Did I achieve my goals for today? If not, did I make progress?

_____

_____

How do I feel now that I have completed (or not completed) this goal?

_____

_____

What three things will you no longer accept?

1. _____
2. _____
3. _____

What are 3 prayers that I have for today?

1. _____
2. _____
3. _____

Today, I release ... _____

_____

I WILL LIVE EACH DAY WITH

purpose.

Day 35

Morning Affirmation

Today, I am grateful for... _____
_____
_____
_____

What I learned from yesterday... _____
_____
_____
_____

As a reminder, my 90-day goal is to..._____
_____
_____

Why is this goal important?_____
_____
_____

Three realistic steps that I can take towards this goal today are...

1. _____
2. _____
3. _____

Day 35

Evening Affirmation

Did I achieve my goals for today? If not, did I make progress?

_____

_____

How do I feel now that I have completed (or not completed) this goal?

_____

_____

What three things will you no longer accept?

1. _____
2. _____
3. _____

What are 3 prayers that I have for today?

1. _____
2. _____
3. _____

Today, I release ... _____

_____

Day 36

Today, I am grateful for... _____

_____

_____

_____

What I learned from yesterday... _____

_____

_____

_____

As a reminder, my 90-day goal is to... _____

_____

_____

Why is this goal important? _____

_____

_____

Three realistic steps that I can take towards this goal today are...

1. _____

2. _____

3. _____

Day 36

Evening Affirmation

Did I achieve my goals for today? If not, did I make progress?

_____

_____

How do I feel now that I have completed (or not completed) this goal?

_____

_____

What three things will you no longer accept?

1. _____
2. _____
3. _____

What are 3 prayers that I have for today?

1. _____
2. _____
3. _____

Today, I release ... _____

_____

I am more

THAN MY PAST

FAILURES.

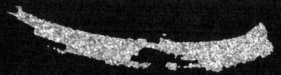

Day 37

Today, I am grateful for... _____

_____

_____

_____

What I learned from yesterday... _____

_____

_____

_____

As a reminder, my 90-day goal is to... _____

_____

_____

Why is this goal important? _____

_____

_____

Three realistic steps that I can take towards this goal today are...

1. _____
2. _____
3. _____

Day 37

Evening Affirmation

Did I achieve my goals for today? If not, did I make progress?

_____

_____

How do I feel now that I have completed (or not completed) this goal?

_____

_____

What three things will you no longer accept?

1. _____
2. _____
3. _____

What are 3 prayers that I have for today?

1. _____
2. _____
3. _____

Today, I release ... _____

_____

Day 38

Today, I am grateful for... _____

_____

_____

_____

What I learned from yesterday... _____

_____

_____

_____

As a reminder, my 90-day goal is to... _____

_____

_____

Why is this goal important? _____

_____

_____

Three realistic steps that I can take towards this goal today are...

1. _____

2. _____

3. _____

Day 38

Did I achieve my goals for today? If not, did I make progress?

_____

_____

How do I feel now that I have completed (or not completed) this goal?

_____

_____

What three things will you no longer accept?

1. _____
2. _____
3. _____

What are 3 prayers that I have for today?

1. _____
2. _____
3. _____

Today, I release ... _____

_____

I ACCEPT THE OLD ME BECAUSE IT BROUGHT ABOUT THE

the new me.

Day 39

Morning Affirmation

Today, I am grateful for... _____

_____

_____

_____

What I learned from yesterday... _____

_____

_____

_____

As a reminder, my 90-day goal is to... _____

_____

_____

Why is this goal important? _____

_____

_____

Three realistic steps that I can take towards this goal today are...

1. _____

2. _____

3. _____

Day 39

Did I achieve my goals for today? If not, did I make progress?

_____

_____

How do I feel now that I have completed (or not completed) this goal?

_____

_____

What three things will you no longer accept?

1. _____
2. _____
3. _____

What are 3 prayers that I have for today?

1. _____
2. _____
3. _____

Today, I release ... _____

_____

Day 40

Today, I am grateful for... _____

_____

_____

_____

What I learned from yesterday... _____

_____

_____

_____

As a reminder, my 90-day goal is to... _____

_____

_____

Why is this goal important? _____

_____

_____

Three realistic steps that I can take towards this goal today are...

1. _____

2. _____

3. _____

Day 40

Evening Affirmation

Did I achieve my goals for today? If not, did I make progress?

_____

_____

How do I feel now that I have completed (or not completed) this goal?

_____

_____

What three things will you no longer accept?

1. _____
2. _____
3. _____

What are 3 prayers that I have for today?

1. _____
2. _____
3. _____

Today, I release ... _____

_____

I am

DEDICATED
TO BECOMING A
BETTER PERSON.

Day 41

Morning Affirmation

Today, I am grateful for... _____

_____

_____

_____

What I learned from yesterday... _____

_____

_____

_____

As a reminder, my 90-day goal is to..._____

_____

_____

Why is this goal important?_____

_____

_____

Three realistic steps that I can take towards this goal today are...

1. _____

2. _____

3. _____

Day 41

Did I achieve my goals for today? If not, did I make progress?

_____

_____

How do I feel now that I have completed (or not completed) this goal?

_____

_____

What three things will you no longer accept?

1. _____
2. _____
3. _____

What are 3 prayers that I have for today?

1. _____
2. _____
3. _____

Today, I release ... _____

_____

Each day,

I AM GETTING CLOSER TO ACHIEVING MY GOALS.

Day 42

Today, I am grateful for... _____

_____

_____

_____

What I learned from yesterday... _____

_____

_____

_____

As a reminder, my 90-day goal is to... _____

_____

_____

Why is this goal important? _____

_____

_____

Three realistic steps that I can take towards this goal today are...

1. _____
2. _____
3. _____

Day 42

Did I achieve my goals for today? If not, did I make progress?

_____

_____

How do I feel now that I have completed (or not completed) this goal?

_____

_____

What three things will you no longer accept?

1. _____

2. _____

3. _____

What are 3 prayers that I have for today?

1. _____

2. _____

3. _____

Today, I release … _____

_____

WHATEVER YOU DO, DO IT FROM YOUR HEART.

Day 43

Today, I am grateful for... _____

_____

_____

_____

What I learned from yesterday... _____

_____

_____

_____

As a reminder, my 90-day goal is to... _____

_____

_____

Why is this goal important? _____

_____

_____

Three realistic steps that I can take towards this goal today are...

1. _____

2. _____

3. _____

Day 43

Did I achieve my goals for today? If not, did I make progress?

_____

_____

How do I feel now that I have completed (or not completed) this goal?

_____

_____

What three things will you no longer accept?

1. _____
2. _____
3. _____

What are 3 prayers that I have for today?

1. _____
2. _____
3. _____

Today, I release ... _____

_____

EVERYDAY, I FIND SOMETHING NEW TO LOVE ABOUT MYSELF.

Day 44

Today, I am grateful for... _____

_____

_____

_____

What I learned from yesterday... _____

_____

_____

_____

As a reminder, my 90-day goal is to... _____

_____

_____

Why is this goal important? _____

_____

_____

Three realistic steps that I can take towards this goal today are...

1. _____
2. _____
3. _____

Day 44

Evening Affirmation

Did I achieve my goals for today? If not, did I make progress?

_____

_____

How do I feel now that I have completed (or not completed) this goal?

_____

_____

What three things will you no longer accept?

1. _____
2. _____
3. _____

What are 3 prayers that I have for today?

1. _____
2. _____
3. _____

Today, I release … _____

_____

I am
CONTINUALLY
EVOLVING INTO
A STRONGER
VERSION OF
MYSELF.

Day 45

Morning Affirmation

Today, I am grateful for... _____
_____
_____
_____

What I learned from yesterday... _____
_____
_____
_____

As a reminder, my 90-day goal is to... _____
_____
_____

Why is this goal important? _____
_____
_____

Three realistic steps that I can take towards this goal today are...

1. _____
2. _____
3. _____

Day 45

Did I achieve my goals for today? If not, did I make progress?

_____

_____

How do I feel now that I have completed (or not completed)
this goal?

_____

_____

What three things will you no longer accept?

1. _____
2. _____
3. _____

What are 3 prayers that I have for today?

1. _____
2. _____
3. _____

Today, I release ... _____

_____

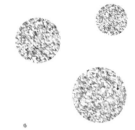

WHATEVER YOU DECIDE TO DO, MAKE SURE IT MAKES YOU HAPPY.

- Paulo Coelho

Day 46

Today, I am grateful for... _____

_____

_____

_____

What I learned from yesterday... _____

_____

_____

_____

As a reminder, my 90-day goal is to... _____

_____

_____

Why is this goal important? _____

_____

_____

Three realistic steps that I can take towards this goal today are...

1. _____

2. _____

3. _____

Day 46

Evening Affirmation

Did I achieve my goals for today? If not, did I make progress?

_____

_____

How do I feel now that I have completed (or not completed) this goal?

_____

_____

What three things will you no longer accept?

1. _____
2. _____
3. _____

What are 3 prayers that I have for today?

1. _____
2. _____
3. _____

Today, I release ... _____

_____

IF YOU WANT TO BE HAPPY, SET A GOAL THAT COMMANDS YOUR THOUGHTS, LIBERATES YOUR ENERGY AND INSPIRES YOUR HOPES.

– Andrew Carnegie

Day 47

Today, I am grateful for... _____
_____
_____
_____

What I learned from yesterday... _____
_____
_____
_____

As a reminder, my 90-day goal is to... _____
_____
_____

Why is this goal important? _____
_____
_____

Three realistic steps that I can take towards this goal today are...

1. _____
2. _____
3. _____

Day 47

Did I achieve my goals for today? If not, did I make progress?

_____

_____

How do I feel now that I have completed (or not completed) this goal?

_____

_____

What three things will you no longer accept?

1. _____
2. _____
3. _____

What are 3 prayers that I have for today?

1. _____
2. _____
3. _____

Today, I release ... _____

_____

FIGHT FOR YOUR JOURNEY!

Day 48

Today, I am grateful for... _____

_____

_____

_____

What I learned from yesterday... _____

_____

_____

_____

As a reminder, my 90-day goal is to... _____

_____

_____

Why is this goal important? _____

_____

_____

Three realistic steps that I can take towards this goal today are...

1. _____

2. _____

3. _____

Day 48

Did I achieve my goals for today? If not, did I make progress?

_____

_____

How do I feel now that I have completed (or not completed) this goal?

_____

_____

What three things will you no longer accept?

1. _____
2. _____
3. _____

What are 3 prayers that I have for today?

1. _____
2. _____
3. _____

Today, I release ... _____

_____

MY ABILITY TO
CONQUER
MY CHALLENGES
IS LIMITLESS;
MY POTENTIAL
TO SUCCEED
IS INFINITE.

- J. IVORY

Day 49

Today, I am grateful for... _____

_____

_____

_____

What I learned from yesterday... _____

_____

_____

_____

As a reminder, my 90-day goal is to... _____

_____

_____

Why is this goal important? _____

_____

_____

Three realistic steps that I can take towards this goal today are...

1. _____
2. _____
3. _____

Day 49

Evening Affirmation

Did I achieve my goals for today? If not, did I make progress?

_____

_____

How do I feel now that I have completed (or not completed) this goal?

_____

_____

What three things will you no longer accept?

1. _____
2. _____
3. _____

What are 3 prayers that I have for today?

1. _____
2. _____
3. _____

Today, I release ... _____

_____

NOTHING ANYONE CAN SAY CAN CHANGE WHAT I THINK ABOUT MYSELF.

Day 50

Today, I am grateful for... _____

_____

_____

_____

What I learned from yesterday... _____

_____

_____

_____

As a reminder, my 90-day goal is to... _____

_____

_____

Why is this goal important? _____

_____

_____

Three realistic steps that I can take towards this goal today are...

1. _____

2. _____

3. _____

Day 50

Evening Affirmation

Did I achieve my goals for today? If not, did I make progress?

_____

_____

How do I feel now that I have completed (or not completed) this goal?

_____

_____

What three things will you no longer accept?
1. _____
2. _____
3. _____

What are 3 prayers that I have for today?
1. _____
2. _____
3. _____

Today, I release ... _____

_____

I HAVE SURVIVED WHAT WAS SUPPOSED TO HARM ME AND DESTROY ME.

Look at me now!

Day 51

Morning Affirmation

Today, I am grateful for... _____

_____

_____

_____

What I learned from yesterday... _____

_____

_____

_____

As a reminder, my 90-day goal is to... _____

_____

_____

Why is this goal important? _____

_____

_____

Three realistic steps that I can take towards this goal today are...
1. _____
2. _____
3. _____

Day 51

Evening Affirmation

Did I achieve my goals for today? If not, did I make progress?

_____

_____

How do I feel now that I have completed (or not completed) this goal?

_____

_____

What three things will you no longer accept?

1. _____

2. _____

3. _____

What are 3 prayers that I have for today?

1. _____

2. _____

3. _____

Today, I release ... _____

_____

I am fully
committed to
achieving
my goals.

Day 52

Today, I am grateful for... _____

_____

_____

_____

What I learned from yesterday... _____

_____

_____

_____

As a reminder, my 90-day goal is to..._____

_____

_____

Why is this goal important? _____

_____

_____

Three realistic steps that I can take towards this goal today are...

1. _____

2. _____

3. _____

Day 52

Evening Affirmation

Did I achieve my goals for today? If not, did I make progress?

_____

_____

How do I feel now that I have completed (or not completed) this goal?

_____

_____

What three things will you no longer accept?

1. _____
2. _____
3. _____

What are 3 prayers that I have for today?

1. _____
2. _____
3. _____

Today, I release ... _____

_____

I CAN
FINALLY SEE MY
BEAUTY,
MY VALUE AND
MY WORTH.

Day 53

Morning Affirmation

Today, I am grateful for... _____

_____

_____

_____

What I learned from yesterday... _____

_____

_____

_____

As a reminder, my 90-day goal is to... _____

_____

_____

Why is this goal important? _____

_____

_____

Three realistic steps that I can take towards this goal today are...

1. _____

2. _____

3. _____

Day 53

Evening Affirmation

Did I achieve my goals for today? If not, did I make progress?

_____

_____

How do I feel now that I have completed (or not completed) this goal?

_____

_____

What three things will you no longer accept?
1. _____
2. _____
3. _____

What are 3 prayers that I have for today?
1. _____
2. _____
3. _____

Today, I release ... _____

_____

I MADE PEACE WITH MY PURPOSE, AND I EMBRACE WHO I AM.

Day 54

Today, I am grateful for... _____

_____

_____

_____

What I learned from yesterday... _____

_____

_____

_____

As a reminder, my 90-day goal is to... _____

_____

_____

Why is this goal important? _____

_____

_____

Three realistic steps that I can take towards this goal today are...

1. _____

2. _____

3. _____

Day 54

Did I achieve my goals for today? If not, did I make progress?

_____

_____

How do I feel now that I have completed (or not completed) this goal?

_____

_____

What three things will you no longer accept?

1. _____
2. _____
3. _____

What are 3 prayers that I have for today?

1. _____
2. _____
3. _____

Today, I release ... _____

_____

WHAT THE ENEMY USES TO HURT YOU GOD USES TO PROSPER YOU.

Day 55

Today, I am grateful for... _____

_____

_____

_____

What I learned from yesterday... _____

_____

_____

_____

As a reminder, my 90-day goal is to... _____

_____

_____

Why is this goal important? _____

_____

_____

Three realistic steps that I can take towards this goal today are...

1. _____

2. _____

3. _____

Day 55

Did I achieve my goals for today? If not, did I make progress?

_____

_____

How do I feel now that I have completed (or not completed) this goal?

_____

_____

What three things will you no longer accept?

1. _____
2. _____
3. _____

What are 3 prayers that I have for today?

1. _____
2. _____
3. _____

Today, I release ... _____

_____

_I am_

CONSTANTLY
SURROUNDED
BY <u>LOVE</u>.

Day 56

Today, I am grateful for... _____
_____
_____
_____

What I learned from yesterday... _____
_____
_____
_____

As a reminder, my 90-day goal is to... _____
_____
_____

Why is this goal important? _____
_____
_____

Three realistic steps that I can take towards this goal today are...

1. _____
2. _____
3. _____

Day 56

Did I achieve my goals for today? If not, did I make progress?

_____

_____

How do I feel now that I have completed (or not completed) this goal?

_____

_____

What three things will you no longer accept?

1. _____
2. _____
3. _____

What are 3 prayers that I have for today?

1. _____
2. _____
3. _____

Today, I release ... _____

_____

IT IS NECESSARY TO DO GOOD THINGS FOR MYSELF.

Day 57

Today, I am grateful for... _____

_____

_____

_____

What I learned from yesterday... _____

_____

_____

_____

As a reminder, my 90-day goal is to... _____

_____

_____

Why is this goal important? _____

_____

_____

Three realistic steps that I can take towards this goal today are...

1. _____

2 _____

3 _____

Day 57

Did I achieve my goals for today? If not, did I make progress?

_____

_____

How do I feel now that I have completed (or not completed) this goal?

_____

_____

What three things will you no longer accept?

1. _____
2. _____
3. _____

What are 3 prayers that I have for today?

1. _____
2. _____
3. _____

Today, I release ... _____

_____

Happiness

ALWAYS COMES FROM WITHIN.

Day 58

Today, I am grateful for... _____

_____

_____

_____

What I learned from yesterday... _____

_____

_____

_____

As a reminder, my 90-day goal is to... _____

_____

_____

Why is this goal important? _____

_____

_____

Three realistic steps that I can take towards this goal today are...

1. _____
2. _____
3. _____

Day 58

Did I achieve my goals for today? If not, did I make progress?

_____

_____

How do I feel now that I have completed (or not completed) this goal?

_____

_____

What three things will you no longer accept?

1. _____
2. _____
3. _____

What are 3 prayers that I have for today?

1. _____
2. _____
3. _____

Today, I release ... _____

_____

Day 59

Today, I am grateful for... _____
_____
_____
_____

What I learned from yesterday... _____
_____
_____
_____

As a reminder, my 90-day goal is to... _____
_____
_____

Why is this goal important? _____
_____
_____

Three realistic steps that I can take towards this goal today are...

1. _____
2. _____
3. _____

Day 59

Evening Affirmation

Did I achieve my goals for today? If not, did I make progress?

_____

_____

How do I feel now that I have completed (or not completed) this goal?

_____

_____

What three things will you no longer accept?

1. _____
2. _____
3. _____

What are 3 prayers that I have for today?

1. _____
2. _____
3. _____

Today, I release … _____

_____

Get up and
WIN!

Day 60

Today, I am grateful for... _____

_____

_____

_____

What I learned from yesterday... _____

_____

_____

_____

As a reminder, my 90-day goal is to... _____

_____

_____

Why is this goal important? _____

_____

_____

Three realistic steps that I can take towards this goal today are...

1. _____

2. _____

3. _____

Day 60

Evening Affirmation

Did I achieve my goals for today? If not, did I make progress?

_____

_____

How do I feel now that I have completed (or not completed) this goal?

_____

_____

What three things will you no longer accept?

1. _____
2. _____
3. _____

What are 3 prayers that I have for today?

1. _____
2. _____
3. _____

Today, I release ... _____

_____

TRYING IS AN EXCUSE TO FAIL!

Make it happen!

Day 61

Today, I am grateful for... _____
_____
_____
_____

What I learned from yesterday... _____
_____
_____
_____

As a reminder, my 90-day goal is to... _____
_____
_____

Why is this goal important? _____
_____
_____

Three realistic steps that I can take towards this goal today are...

1. _____
2. _____
3. _____

Day 61

Did I achieve my goals for today? If not, did I make progress?

_____

_____

How do I feel now that I have completed (or not completed) this goal?

_____

_____

What three things will you no longer accept?

1. _____
2. _____
3. _____

What are 3 prayers that I have for today?

1. _____
2. _____
3. _____

Today, I release ... _____

_____

Day 62

Morning Affirmation

Today, I am grateful for... _____

_____

_____

_____

What I learned from yesterday... _____

_____

_____

_____

As a reminder, my 90-day goal is to... _____

_____

_____

Why is this goal important? _____

_____

_____

Three realistic steps that I can take towards this goal today are...

1. _____

2. _____

3. _____

Day 62

Did I achieve my goals for today? If not, did I make progress?

_____

_____

How do I feel now that I have completed (or not completed) this goal?

_____

_____

What three things will you no longer accept?

1. _____
2. _____
3. _____

What are 3 prayers that I have for today?

1. _____
2. _____
3. _____

Today, I release ... _____

_____

CONGRATULATE YOURSELF ON THE PROCESS THAT NO ONE KNOWS ABOUT.

Day 63

Morning Affirmation

Today, I am grateful for... _____
_____
_____
_____

What I learned from yesterday... _____
_____
_____
_____

As a reminder, my 90-day goal is to... _____
_____
_____

Why is this goal important? _____
_____
_____

Three realistic steps that I can take towards this goal today are...

1. _____
2. _____
3. _____

Day 63

Did I achieve my goals for today? If not, did I make progress?

_____

_____

How do I feel now that I have completed (or not completed)
this goal?

_____

_____

What three things will you no longer accept?

1. _____
2. _____
3. _____

What are 3 prayers that I have for today?

1. _____
2. _____
3. _____

Today, I release ... _____

_____

I am proud
OF MYSELF!

Day 64

Today, I am grateful for... _____
_____
_____
_____

What I learned from yesterday... _____
_____
_____
_____

As a reminder, my 90-day goal is to..._____
_____
_____

Why is this goal important?_____
_____
_____

Three realistic steps that I can take towards this goal today are...

1. _____
2. _____
3. _____

Day 64

Did I achieve my goals for today? If not, did I make progress?

_____

_____

How do I feel now that I have completed (or not completed) this goal?

_____

_____

What three things will you no longer accept?

1. _____

2. _____

3. _____

What are 3 prayers that I have for today?

1. _____

2. _____

3. _____

Today, I release ... _____

_____

Overthinking

WILL STEAL YOUR PEACE AND SLEEP. PRAY AND LEAVE IT IN GOD'S HANDS.

Day 65

Today, I am grateful for... _____
_____
_____
_____

What I learned from yesterday... _____
_____
_____
_____

As a reminder, my 90-day goal is to... _____
_____
_____

Why is this goal important? _____
_____
_____

Three realistic steps that I can take towards this goal today are...

1. _____
2. _____
3. _____

Day 65

Evening Affirmation

Did I achieve my goals for today? If not, did I make progress?

_____

_____

How do I feel now that I have completed (or not completed) this goal?

_____

_____

What three things will you no longer accept?

1. _____
2. _____
3. _____

What are 3 prayers that I have for today?

1. _____
2. _____
3. _____

Today, I release ... _____

_____

IT IS NECESSARY TO DO GOOD THINGS FOR MYSELF.

Day 66

Today, I am grateful for... _____

_____

_____

_____

What I learned from yesterday... _____

_____

_____

_____

As a reminder, my 90-day goal is to..._____

_____

_____

Why is this goal important?_____

_____

_____

Three realistic steps that I can take towards this goal today are...

1. _____

2. _____

3. _____

Day 66

Did I achieve my goals for today? If not, did I make progress?

_____

_____

How do I feel now that I have completed (or not completed) this goal?

_____

_____

What three things will you no longer accept?

1. _____
2. _____
3. _____

What are 3 prayers that I have for today?

1. _____
2. _____
3. _____

Today, I release ... _____

_____

I AM MORE THAN

a conqueror!

Day 67

Today, I am grateful for... _____

_____

_____

_____

What I learned from yesterday... _____

_____

_____

_____

As a reminder, my 90-day goal is to... _____

_____

_____

Why is this goal important? _____

_____

_____

Three realistic steps that I can take towards this goal today are...

1. _____

2. _____

3. _____

Day 67

Evening Affirmation

Did I achieve my goals for today? If not, did I make progress?

_____

_____

How do I feel now that I have completed (or not completed) this goal?

_____

_____

What three things will you no longer accept?

1. _____
2. _____
3. _____

What are 3 prayers that I have for today?

1. _____
2. _____
3. _____

Today, I release ... _____

_____

Love
NEVER FAILS!

Day 68

Today, I am grateful for... _____

_____

_____

_____

What I learned from yesterday... _____

_____

_____

_____

As a reminder, my 90-day goal is to... _____

_____

_____

Why is this goal important? _____

_____

_____

Three realistic steps that I can take towards this goal today are...

1. _____

2. _____

3. _____

Day 68

Did I achieve my goals for today? If not, did I make progress?

_____

_____

How do I feel now that I have completed (or not completed) this goal?

_____

_____

What three things will you no longer accept?

1. _____

2. _____

3. _____

What are 3 prayers that I have for today?

1. _____

2. _____

3. _____

Today, I release ... _____

_____

EVERY DAY, I MAKE IT A HABIT TO FEEL AND BE

grateful.

Day 69

Today, I am grateful for... _____
_____
_____
_____

What I learned from yesterday... _____
_____
_____
_____

As a reminder, my 90-day goal is to..._____
_____
_____

Why is this goal important?_____
_____
_____

Three realistic steps that I can take towards this goal today are...

1. _____
2. _____
3. _____

Day 69

Did I achieve my goals for today? If not, did I make progress?

_____

_____

How do I feel now that I have completed (or not completed) this goal?

_____

_____

What three things will you no longer accept?

1. _____
2. _____
3. _____

What are 3 prayers that I have for today?

1. _____
2. _____
3. _____

Today, I release ... _____

_____

Pain

IS TEMPORARY.

Day 70

Today, I am grateful for... _____

_____

_____

_____

What I learned from yesterday... _____

_____

_____

_____

As a reminder, my 90-day goal is to... _____

_____

_____

Why is this goal important? _____

_____

_____

Three realistic steps that I can take towards this goal today are...

1. _____
2. _____
3. _____

Day 70

Did I achieve my goals for today? If not, did I make progress?

_____

_____

How do I feel now that I have completed (or not completed) this goal?

_____

_____

What three things will you no longer accept?

1. _____
2. _____
3. _____

What are 3 prayers that I have for today?

1. _____
2. _____
3. _____

Today, I release ... _____

_____

MOVE
WITH
COMPASSION.

Day 71

Today, I am grateful for... _____
_____
_____
_____

What I learned from yesterday... _____
_____
_____
_____

As a reminder, my 90-day goal is to... _____
_____
_____

Why is this goal important? _____
_____
_____

Three realistic steps that I can take towards this goal today are...

1 _____
2 _____
3 _____

Day 71

Evening Affirmation

Did I achieve my goals for today? If not, did I make progress?

_____

_____

How do I feel now that I have completed (or not completed)
this goal?

_____

_____

What three things will you no longer accept?

1. _____
2. _____
3. _____

What are 3 prayers that I have for today?

1. _____
2. _____
3. _____

Today, I release ... _____

_____

SOMETIMES, THE BRAVEST AND MOST IMPORTANT THING YOU CAN DO IS JUST SHOW UP.

Day 72

Today, I am grateful for... _____
_____
_____
_____

What I learned from yesterday... _____
_____
_____
_____

As a reminder, my 90-day goal is to... _____
_____
_____

Why is this goal important? _____
_____
_____

Three realistic steps that I can take towards this goal today are...

1. _____
2. _____
3. _____

Day 72

Evening Affirmation

Did I achieve my goals for today? If not, did I make progress?

_____

_____

How do I feel now that I have completed (or not completed) this goal?

_____

_____

What three things will you no longer accept?

1. _____
2. _____
3. _____

What are 3 prayers that I have for today?

1. _____
2. _____
3. _____

Today, I release ... _____

_____

BEAUTY BEGINS THE MOMENT YOU DECIDE TO BE YOURSELF.

— *Coco Chanel*

Day 73

Morning Affirmation

Today, I am grateful for... _____

_____

_____

_____

What I learned from yesterday... _____

_____

_____

_____

As a reminder, my 90-day goal is to... _____

_____

_____

Why is this goal important? _____

_____

_____

Three realistic steps that I can take towards this goal today are...

1. _____
2. _____
3. _____

Day 73

Did I achieve my goals for today? If not, did I make progress?

_____

_____

How do I feel now that I have completed (or not completed) this goal?

_____

_____

What three things will you no longer accept?

1. _____
2. _____
3. _____

What are 3 prayers that I have for today?

1. _____
2. _____
3. _____

Today, I release ... _____

_____

It`s my life

- LIVE IT WELL!

Day 74

Today, I am grateful for... _____

_____

_____

_____

What I learned from yesterday... _____

_____

_____

_____

As a reminder, my 90-day goal is to... _____

_____

_____

Why is this goal important? _____

_____

_____

Three realistic steps that I can take towards this goal today are...

1. _____
2. _____
3. _____

Day 74

Did I achieve my goals for today? If not, did I make progress?

_____

_____

How do I feel now that I have completed (or not completed) this goal?

_____

_____

What three things will you no longer accept?

1. _____

2. _____

3. _____

What are 3 prayers that I have for today?

1. _____

2. _____

3. _____

Today, I release ... _____

_____

LET YOUR DREAMS BE BIGGER THAN YOUR FEARS, YOUR ACTIONS LOUDER THAN YOUR WORDS AND YOUR FAITH STRONGER THAN YOUR FEELINGS.

— Unknown.

Day 75

Today, I am grateful for... _____

_____

_____

_____

What I learned from yesterday... _____

_____

_____

_____

As a reminder, my 90-day goal is to... _____

_____

_____

Why is this goal important? _____

_____

_____

Three realistic steps that I can take towards this goal today are...

1. _____
2. _____
3. _____

Day 75

Evening Affirmation

Did I achieve my goals for today? If not, did I make progress?

_____

_____

How do I feel now that I have completed (or not completed)
this goal?

_____

_____

What three things will you no longer accept?

1. _____
2. _____
3. _____

What are 3 prayers that I have for today?

1. _____
2. _____
3. _____

Today, I release ... _____

_____

TAKING CARE OF YOURSELF MAKES YOU STRONGER FOR EVERYONE IN YOUR LIFE....

Including you.

- KELLY RUDOLPH.

Day 76

Today, I am grateful for... _____

_____

_____

_____

What I learned from yesterday... _____

_____

_____

_____

As a reminder, my 90-day goal is to... _____

_____

_____

Why is this goal important? _____

_____

_____

Three realistic steps that I can take towards this goal today are...

1. _____

2. _____

3. _____

Day 76

Did I achieve my goals for today? If not, did I make progress?

_____

_____

How do I feel now that I have completed (or not completed) this goal?

_____

_____

What three things will you no longer accept?

1. _____
2. _____
3. _____

What are 3 prayers that I have for today?

1. _____
2. _____
3. _____

Today, I release ... _____

_____

THE KEY TO SUCCESS IS TO FOCUS ON

the goal,

NOT THE OBSTACLES.

Day 77

Today, I am grateful for... _____

_____

_____

_____

What I learned from yesterday... _____

_____

_____

_____

As a reminder, my 90-day goal is to..._____

_____

_____

Why is this goal important? _____

_____

_____

Three realistic steps that I can take towards this goal today are...

1. _____

2. _____

3. _____

Day 77

Evening Affirmation

Did I achieve my goals for today? If not, did I make progress?

_____

_____

How do I feel now that I have completed (or not completed) this goal?

_____

_____

What three things will you no longer accept?

1. _____
2. _____
3. _____

What are 3 prayers that I have for today?

1. _____
2. _____
3. _____

Today, I release ... _____

_____

DON'T WAIT FOR OPPORTUNITY.

Create it.

Day 78

Today, I am grateful for... _____

_____

_____

_____

What I learned from yesterday... _____

_____

_____

_____

As a reminder, my 90-day goal is to... _____

_____

_____

Why is this goal important? _____

_____

_____

Three realistic steps that I can take towards this goal today are...

1. _____

2. _____

3. _____

Day 78

Did I achieve my goals for today? If not, did I make progress?

_____

_____

How do I feel now that I have completed (or not completed) this goal?

_____

_____

What three things will you no longer accept?

1. _____

2. _____

3. _____

What are 3 prayers that I have for today?

1. _____

2. _____

3. _____

Today, I release ... _____

_____

SUCCESS IS NOT FINAL; FAILURE IS NOT FATAL. IT IS THE COURAGE TO CONTINUE THAT COUNTS.

Winston S. Churchill

Day 79

Today, I am grateful for... _____
_____
_____
_____

What I learned from yesterday... _____
_____
_____
_____

As a reminder, my 90-day goal is to... _____
_____
_____
_____

Why is this goal important? _____
_____
_____

Three realistic steps that I can take towards this goal today are...

1. _____
2. _____
3. _____

Day 79

Did I achieve my goals for today? If not, did I make progress?

_____

_____

How do I feel now that I have completed (or not completed) this goal?

_____

_____

What three things will you no longer accept?

1. _____
2. _____
3. _____

What are 3 prayers that I have for today?

1. _____
2. _____
3. _____

Today, I release ... _____

_____

Day 80

Morning Affirmation

Today, I am grateful for... _____

_____

_____

_____

What I learned from yesterday... _____

_____

_____

_____

As a reminder, my 90-day goal is to... _____

_____

_____

Why is this goal important? _____

_____

_____

Three realistic steps that I can take towards this goal today are...

1. _____

2. _____

3. _____

Day 80

Evening Affirmation

Did I achieve my goals for today? If not, did I make progress?

_____

_____

How do I feel now that I have completed (or not completed) this goal?

_____

_____

What three things will you no longer accept?

1. _____
2. _____
3. _____

What are 3 prayers that I have for today?

1. _____
2. _____
3. _____

Today, I release ... _____

_____

I think

I SHOULD JUST GO FOR IT!

Day 81

Today, I am grateful for... _____
_____
_____
_____

What I learned from yesterday... _____
_____
_____
_____

As a reminder, my 90-day goal is to... _____
_____
_____

Why is this goal important? _____
_____
_____

Three realistic steps that I can take towards this goal today are...

1. _____
2. _____
3. _____

Day 81

Did I achieve my goals for today? If not, did I make progress?

_____

_____

How do I feel now that I have completed (or not completed) this goal?

_____

_____

What three things will you no longer accept?

1. _____
2. _____
3. _____

What are 3 prayers that I have for today?

1. _____
2. _____
3. _____

Today, I release ... _____

_____

Write

the vision.

Day 82

Today, I am grateful for... _____
_____
_____
_____

What I learned from yesterday... _____
_____
_____
_____

As a reminder, my 90-day goal is to..._____
_____
_____
_____

Why is this goal important?_____
_____
_____

Three realistic steps that I can take towards this goal today are...

1. _____
2. _____
3. _____

Day 82

Did I achieve my goals for today? If not, did I make progress?

_____

_____

How do I feel now that I have completed (or not completed) this goal?

_____

_____

What three things will you no longer accept?

1. _____
2. _____
3. _____

What are 3 prayers that I have for today?

1. _____
2. _____
3. _____

Today, I release ... _____

_____

Personal growth

and development

ARE IMPORTANT
TO ME.

Day 83

Today, I am grateful for... _____

_____

_____

_____

What I learned from yesterday... _____

_____

_____

_____

As a reminder, my 90-day goal is to... _____

_____

_____

Why is this goal important? _____

_____

_____

Three realistic steps that I can take towards this goal today are...

1. _____

2. _____

3. _____

Day 83

Evening Affirmation

Did I achieve my goals for today? If not, did I make progress?

_____

_____

How do I feel now that I have completed (or not completed) this goal?

_____

_____

What three things will you no longer accept?

1. _____
2. _____
3. _____

What are 3 prayers that I have for today?

1. _____
2. _____
3. _____

Today, I release ... _____

_____

MY FEELINGS DESERVE TO BE EXPRESSED. I ALLOW THEM TO FLOW.

Day 84

Today, I am grateful for... _____

_____

_____

_____

What I learned from yesterday... _____

_____

_____

_____

As a reminder, my 90-day goal is to... _____

_____

_____

Why is this goal important? _____

_____

_____

Three realistic steps that I can take towards this goal today are...

1. _____

2. _____

3. _____

Day 84

Did I achieve my goals for today? If not, did I make progress?

_____

_____

How do I feel now that I have completed (or not completed) this goal?

_____

_____

What three things will you no longer accept?

1. _____
2. _____
3. _____

What are 3 prayers that I have for today?

1. _____
2. _____
3. _____

Today, I release ... _____

_____

THE BETTER
I FEEL,
THE MORE

I am calm.

Day 85

Today, I am grateful for... _____

_____

_____

_____

What I learned from yesterday... _____

_____

_____

_____

As a reminder, my 90-day goal is to... _____

_____

_____

Why is this goal important? _____

_____

_____

Three realistic steps that I can take towards this goal today are...

1. _____
2. _____
3. _____

Day 85

Evening Affirmation

Did I achieve my goals for today? If not, did I make progress?

_____

_____

How do I feel now that I have completed (or not completed) this goal?

_____

_____

What three things will you no longer accept?

1. _____
2. _____
3. _____

What are 3 prayers that I have for today?

1. _____
2. _____
3. _____

Today, I release ... _____

_____

I ADORE EVERY

unique

QUALITY THAT MAKES ME WHO I AM.

Day 86

Morning Affirmation

Today, I am grateful for... _____

_____

_____

_____

What I learned from yesterday... _____

_____

_____

_____

As a reminder, my 90-day goal is to... _____

_____

_____

Why is this goal important? _____

_____

_____

Three realistic steps that I can take towards this goal today are...

1. _____

2. _____

3. _____

Day 86

Did I achieve my goals for today? If not, did I make progress?

_____

_____

How do I feel now that I have completed (or not completed) this goal?

_____

_____

What three things will you no longer accept?

1. _____
2. _____
3. _____

What are 3 prayers that I have for today?

1. _____
2. _____
3. _____

Today, I release ... _____

_____

Day 87

Today, I am grateful for... _____
_____
_____
_____

What I learned from yesterday... _____
_____
_____
_____

As a reminder, my 90-day goal is to..._____
_____
_____

Why is this goal important?_____
_____
_____

Three realistic steps that I can take towards this goal today are...

1. _____
2. _____
3. _____

Day 87

Did I achieve my goals for today? If not, did I make progress?

_____

_____

How do I feel now that I have completed (or not completed) this goal?

_____

_____

What three things will you no longer accept?

1. _____
2. _____
3. _____

What are 3 prayers that I have for today?

1. _____
2. _____
3. _____

Today, I release ... _____

_____

I AM MY OWN BIGGEST SUPPORTER.

Day 88

Today, I am grateful for... _____

_____

_____

_____

What I learned from yesterday... _____

_____

_____

_____

As a reminder, my 90-day goal is to... _____

_____

_____

Why is this goal important? _____

_____

_____

Three realistic steps that I can take towards this goal today are...

1. _____
2. _____
3. _____

Day 88

Did I achieve my goals for today? If not, did I make progress?

_____

_____

How do I feel now that I have completed (or not completed) this goal?

_____

_____

What three things will you no longer accept?

1. _____
2. _____
3. _____

What are 3 prayers that I have for today?

1. _____
2. _____
3. _____

Today, I release ... _____

_____

I AM CREATING THE LIFE

I deserve.

Day 89

Today, I am grateful for... _____
_____
_____
_____

What I learned from yesterday... _____
_____
_____
_____

As a reminder, my 90-day goal is to..._____
_____
_____

Why is this goal important?_____
_____
_____

Three realistic steps that I can take towards this goal today are...

1. _____
2. _____
3. _____

Day 89

Did I achieve my goals for today? If not, did I make progress?

_____

_____

How do I feel now that I have completed (or not completed) this goal?

_____

_____

What three things will you no longer accept?

1. _____
2. _____
3. _____

What are 3 prayers that I have for today?

1. _____
2. _____
3. _____

Today, I release ... _____

_____

REMEMBER -
WHEN YOU FORGIVE,
YOU HEAL.
AND WHEN YOU
LET GO, YOU

grow.

Day 90

Today, I am grateful for... _____

_____

_____

_____

What I learned from yesterday... _____

_____

_____

_____

As a reminder, my 90-day goal is to... _____

_____

_____

Why is this goal important? _____

_____

_____

Three realistic steps that I can take towards this goal today are...

1. _____

2. _____

3. _____

Day 90

Did I achieve my goals for today? If not, did I make progress?

_____

_____

How do I feel now that I have completed (or not completed) this goal?

_____

_____

What three things will you no longer accept?

1. _____
2. _____
3. _____

What are 3 prayers that I have for today?

1. _____
2. _____
3. _____

Today, I release ... _____

_____

CPSIA information can be obtained
at www.ICGtesting.com
Printed in the USA
BVHW051941300921
617793BV00011B/454